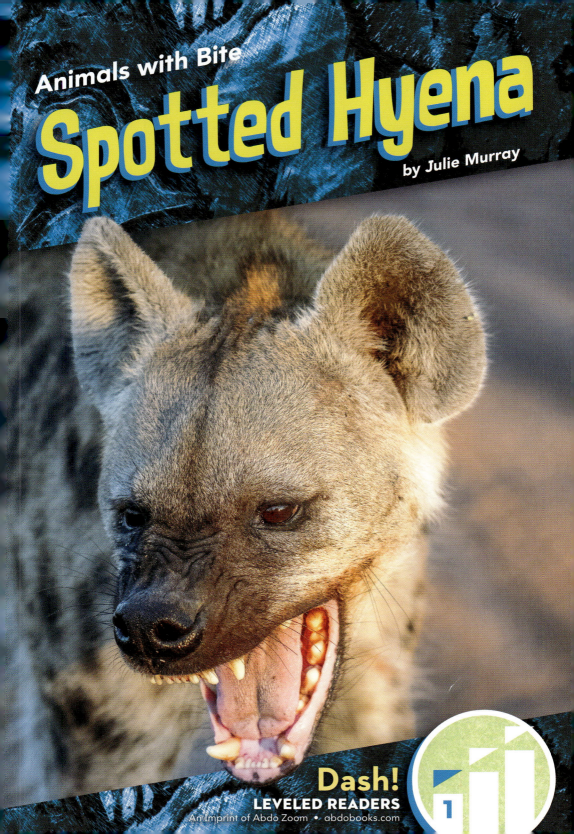

Animals with Bite
Spotted Hyena
by Julie Murray

Dash! LEVELED READERS
An Imprint of Abdo Zoom • abdobooks.com

Level 1 – Beginning
Short and simple sentences with familiar words or patterns for children who are beginning to understand how letters and sounds go together.

Level 2 – Emerging
Longer words and sentences with more complex language patterns for readers who are practicing common words and letter sounds.

Level 3 – Transitional
More developed language and vocabulary for readers who are becoming more independent.

abdobooks.com

Published by Abdo Zoom, a division of ABDO, PO Box 398166, Minneapolis, Minnesota 55439. Copyright © 2021 by Abdo Consulting Group, Inc. International copyrights reserved in all countries. No part of this book may be reproduced in any form without written permission from the publisher. Dash!™ is a trademark and logo of Abdo Zoom.

Printed in the United States of America, North Mankato, Minnesota.
102020
012021

Photo Credits: iStock, Shutterstock
Production Contributors: Kenny Abdo, Jennie Forsberg, Grace Hansen, John Hansen
Design Contributors: Dorothy Toth, Neil Klinepier

Library of Congress Control Number: 2020910922

Publisher's Cataloging in Publication Data

Names: Murray, Julie, author.
Title: Spotted hyena / by Julie Murray
Description: Minneapolis, Minnesota : Abdo Zoom, 2021 | Series: Animals with bite | Includes online resources and index.
Identifiers: ISBN 9781098223021 (lib. bdg.) | ISBN 9781098223724 (ebook) | ISBN 9781098224073 (Read-to-Me ebook)
Subjects: LCSH: Spotted hyena--Juvenile literature. | Hyenas--Juvenile literature. | Spotted hyena--Behavior--Juvenile literature. | Bites and stings--Juvenile literature. | Predatory animals--Juvenile literature.
Classification: DDC 591.53--dc23

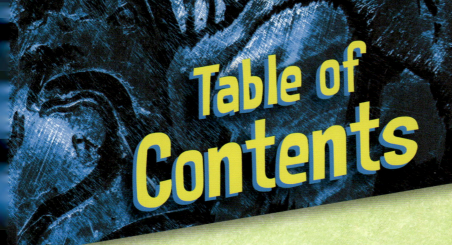

Table of Contents

Spotted Hyena 4
More Facts 22
Glossary 23
Index 24
Online Resources 24

Spotted Hyena

Spotted hyenas live in Africa. It is hot and **dry** there.

They roam grasslands, deserts, and woodlands.

Spotted hyenas have tan fur with dark spots. Their faces are dark in color.

Spotted hyenas are the largest hyena **species**. They can be 3 feet (0.9 m) tall at the shoulders. They weigh up to 180 pounds (81 kg).

Spotted hyenas are often called "laughing hyenas." Their calling noises sound like human laughter!

Spotted hyenas live in large groups called clans. Clans can have up to 80 members.

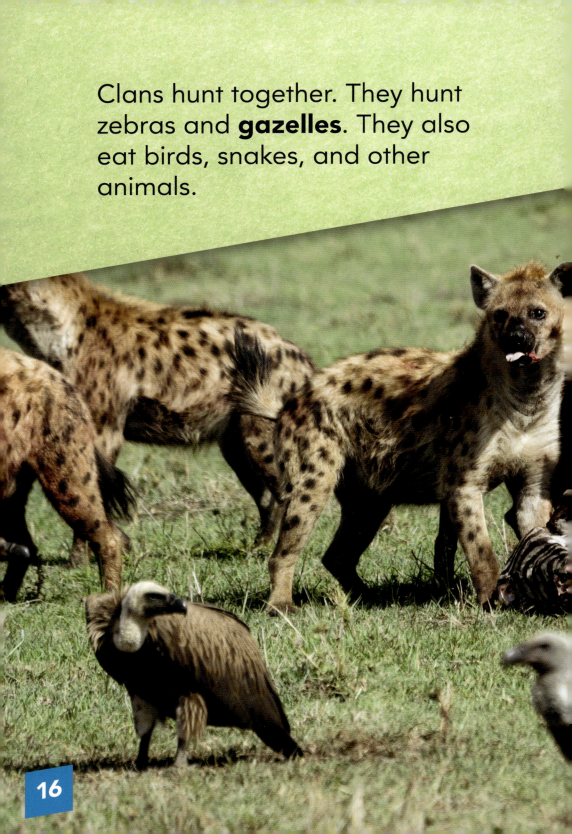

Clans hunt together. They hunt zebras and **gazelles**. They also eat birds, snakes, and other animals.

Spotted hyenas are **scavengers** too!

They have powerful bites! Their sharp teeth can crush bones!

More Facts

- Spotted hyenas are loud animals. They can be heard up to three miles (4.8 km) away!

- They can run more than 35 mph (56 kph)!

- Spotted hyena clans are led by females.

Glossary

dry – having little or no rain.

gazelle – a kind of antelope found in Africa and Asia. It is a mammal with hooves and long legs.

scavenger – an animal that finds and eats dead animals.

species – a group of living things that have similar characteristics and share a common name.

Index

Africa 4
body 8, 11
color 8
food 16, 18
fur 8
groups 14
habitat 4, 6

hunting 16
jaws 21
size 11
sounds 13
teeth 21

Online Resources

Booklinks
NONFICTION NETWORK
FREE! ONLINE NONFICTION RESOURCES

To learn more about spotted hyenas, please visit **abdobooklinks.com** or scan this QR code. These links are routinely monitored and updated to provide the most current information available.